USA State Maps Coloring Book

50 USA States and Territories
Blank, Outline Maps for
Coloring and Education

Updated for 2019
PHOTOCOPYING OK
Ok to Photocopy for Sharing

Detailed Maps

Blank, Outline Maps

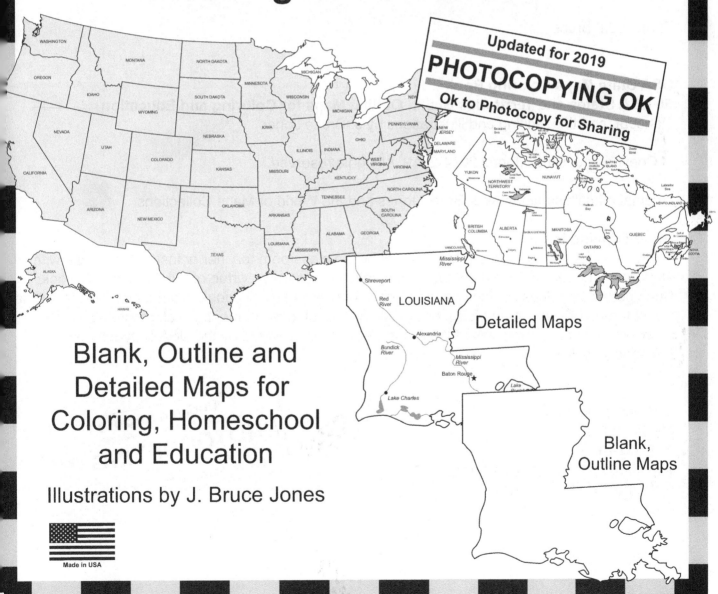

Blank, Outline and Detailed Maps for Coloring, Homeschool and Education

Illustrations by J. Bruce Jones

Made in USA

Dear Reader,

Thank you for buying the USA State Maps Coloring Book. I hope you have fun with it and it proves useful for your students and yourself. I had a lot of fun drawing and creating all of these maps. As I drew them I would image going to all of these amazing places. I love maps and have been drawing them for years. Photocopying this book is completely cool for your students and yourself. So dive in and start coloring.

Thank you, Bruce

USA State Maps Coloring Book
50 USA States and Territories Blank, Outline Maps for Coloring and Education
Concept, creating, editing and illustrations by J. Bruce Jones

Original map illustrations by J. Bruce Jones and the World of Maps Collections

Photocopying is OK

J. Bruce Jones
Mystic, CT
781-492-0742
www.freeusandworldmaps.com
www.mapsfordesign.com

USA State Maps Coloring Book

United States of America

2

United States of America

3

United States of America

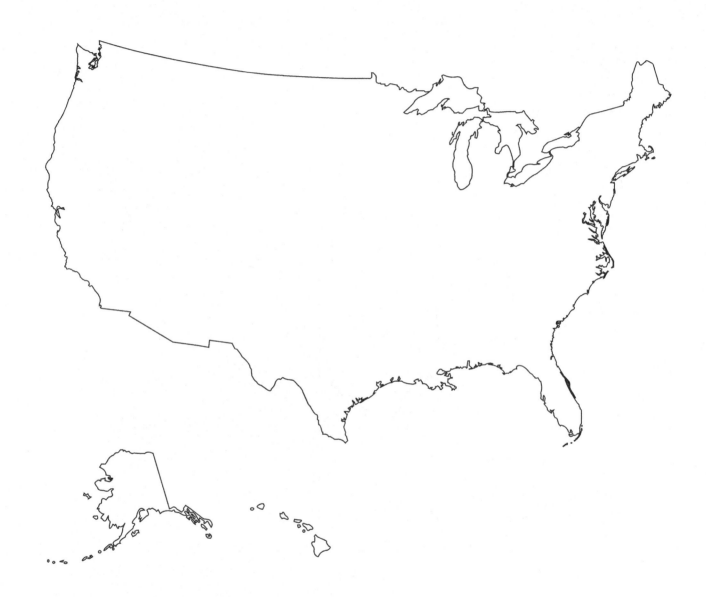

North America

5

North America

Canada

7

Canada

8

Canada

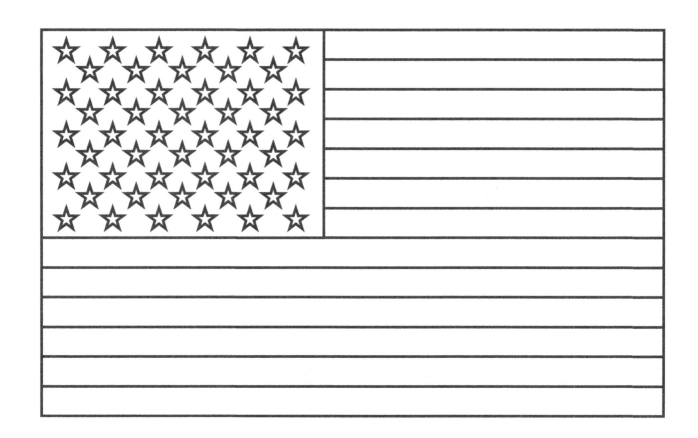

UNITED STATES
of AMERICA

50 USA States

and Territories

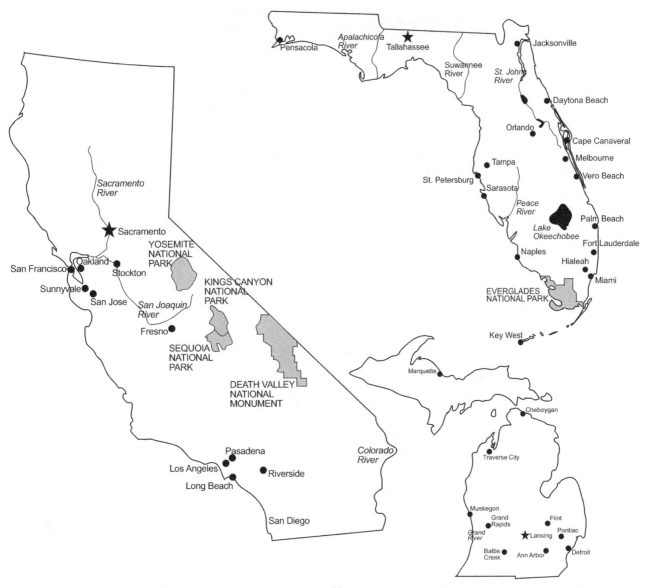

11

Alabama

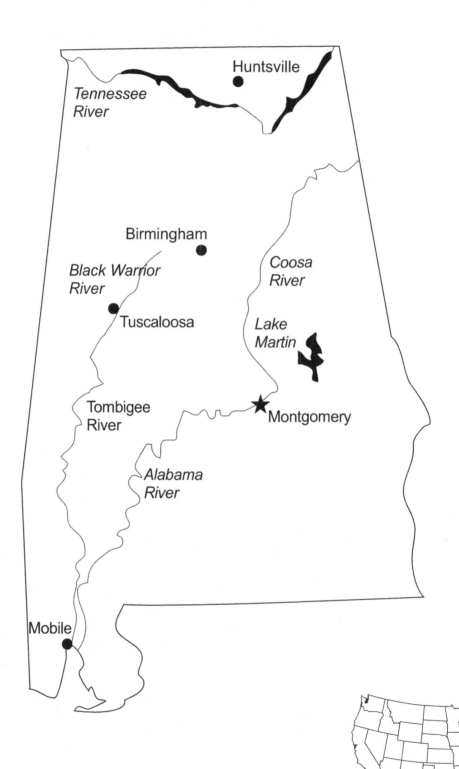

Huntsville

Tennessee River

Birmingham

Black Warrior River

Coosa River

Tuscaloosa

Lake Martin

Tombigee River

★ Montgomery

Alabama River

Mobile

Entered the Union
December 14, 1819

12

Alabama

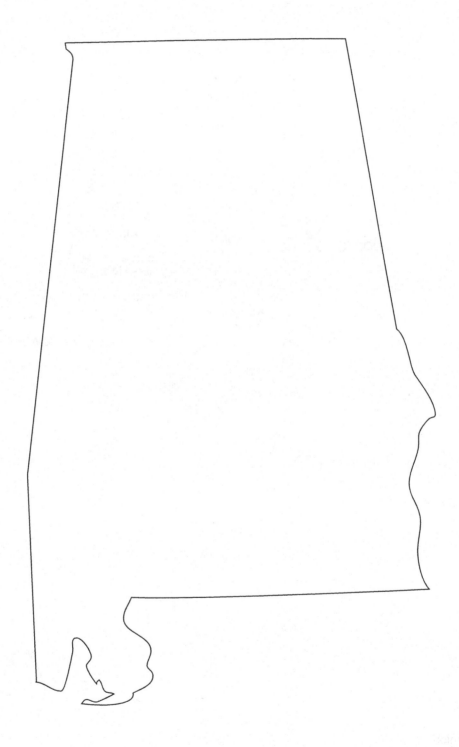

13

Alaska

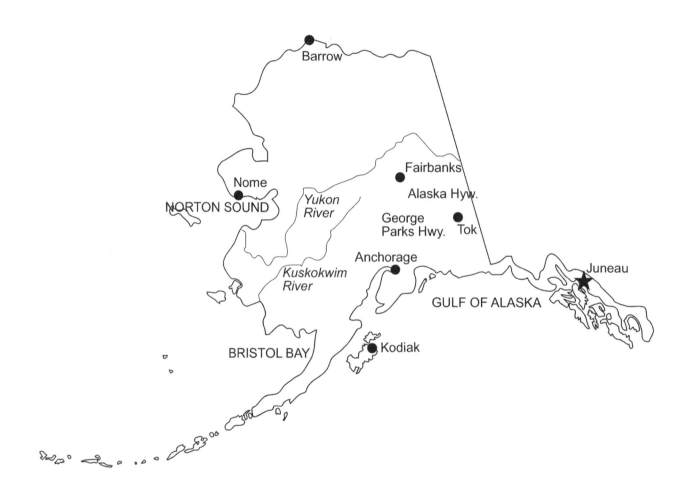

Barrow

Fairbanks

Alaska Hyw.

Nome

NORTON SOUND

Yukon River

George Parks Hwy.   Tok

Kuskokwim River

Anchorage

Juneau

GULF OF ALASKA

BRISTOL BAY

Kodiak

Entered the Union
January 3, 1959

14

Alaska

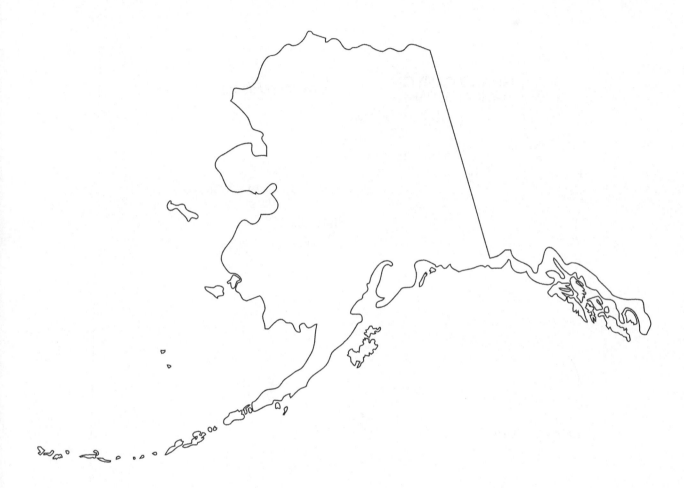

15

Arizona

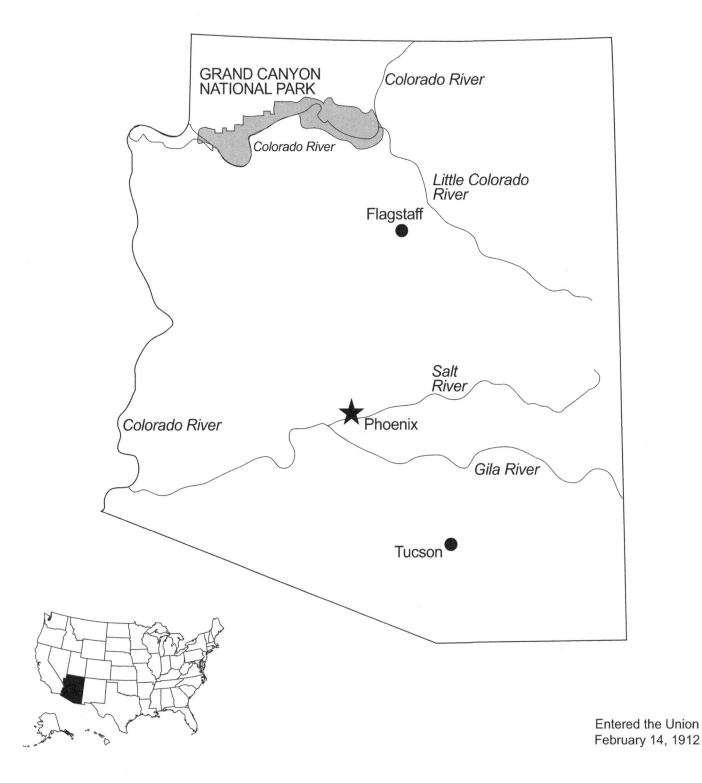

GRAND CANYON
NATIONAL PARK

Colorado River

Colorado River

*Little Colorado
River*

Flagstaff ●

★ Phoenix

*Salt
River*

Colorado River

Gila River

Tucson ●

Entered the Union
February 14, 1912

16

Arizona

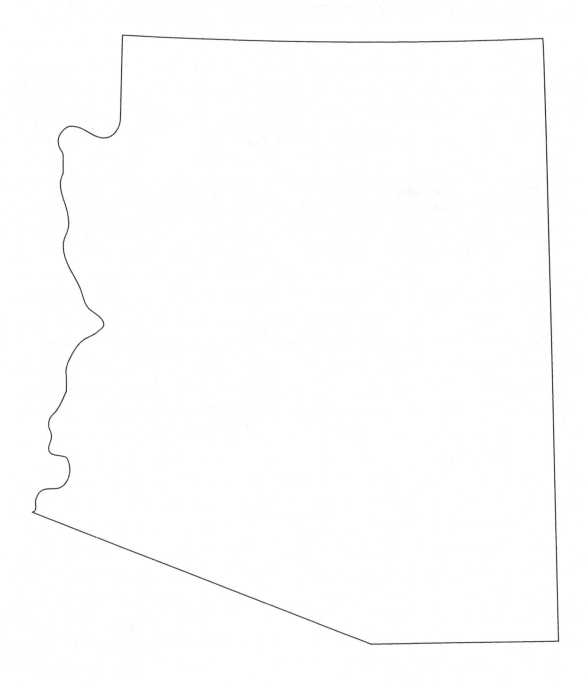

Arkansas

Eleven Point River

White River

Fort Smith

Arkansas River

★ Little Rock

Pine Bluff

Texarkana

Ouachita River

Mississippi River

Entered the Union
June 15, 1836

18

Arkansas

19

California

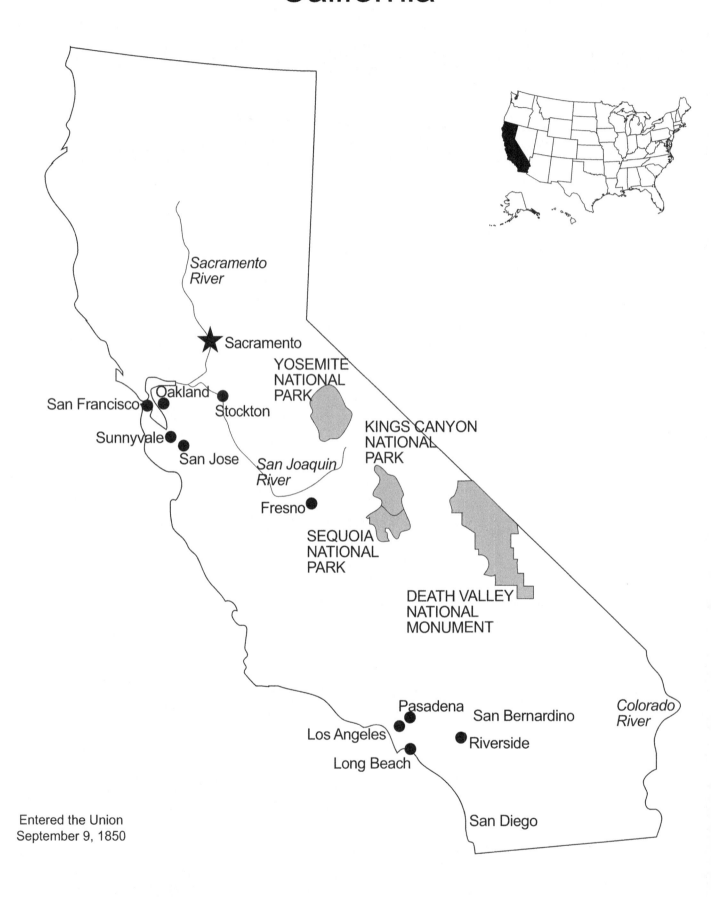

Sacramento River

★ Sacramento

YOSEMITE NATIONAL PARK

San Francisco ● Oakland ● Stockton

KINGS CANYON NATIONAL PARK

Sunnyvale ●
San Jose ●

San Joaquin River

Fresno ●

SEQUOIA NATIONAL PARK

DEATH VALLEY NATIONAL MONUMENT

Pasadena ●
Los Angeles ●

San Bernardino

Colorado River

● Riverside

Long Beach ●

San Diego

Entered the Union
September 9, 1850

California

21

Colorado

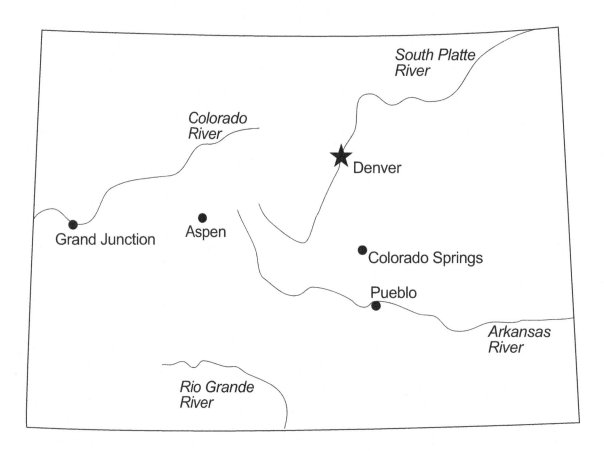

22

Colorado

23

Connecticut

Torrington

Hartford ★

Housatonic River

Waterbury

Meriden

Connecticut River

Norwich

Thames River

Danbury

Housatonic River

New Haven

New London

Bridgeport

Norwalk

Stamford

Entered the Union
January 9, 1788

24

Connecticut

25

Delaware

Wilmington

★ Dover

Delaware
Bay

Entered the Union
December 7, 1787

Delaware

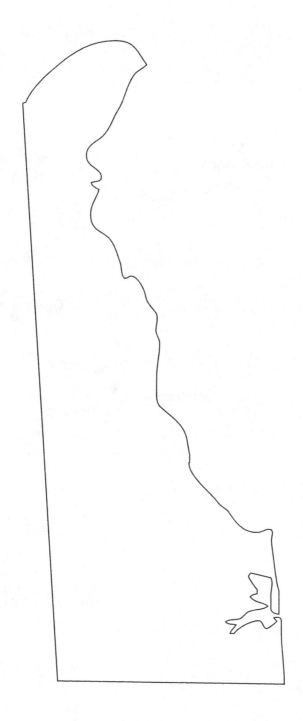

27

Florida

Pensacola

Apalachicola River

Tallahassee

Jacksonville

Suwannee River

St. Johns River

Daytona Beach

Orlando

Cape Canaveral

Melbourne

Tampa

Vero Beach

St. Petersburg

Sarasota

Peace River

Palm Beach

Lake Okeechobee

Fort Lauderdale

Naples

Hialeah

Miami

EVERGLADES
NATIONAL PARK

Key West

Entered the Union
March 3, 1845

28

Florida

29

Georgia

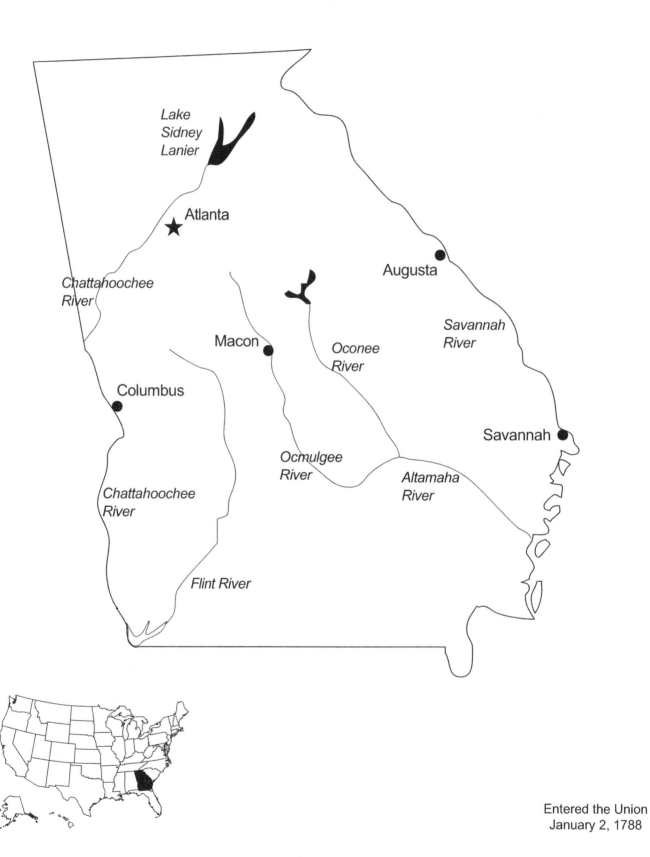

Lake Sidney Lanier

Atlanta

Augusta

Chattahoochee River

Savannah River

Macon

Oconee River

Columbus

Chattahoochee River

Ocmulgee River

Altamaha River

Savannah

Flint River

Entered the Union
January 2, 1788

Georgia

Hawaii

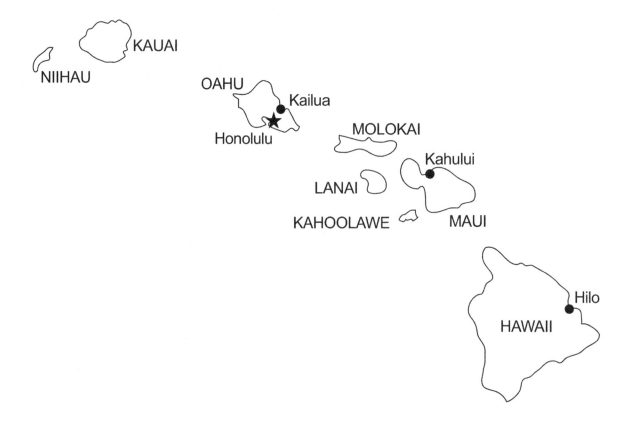

KAUAI

NIIHAU

OAHU

Kailua

Honolulu

MOLOKAI

LANAI

Kahului

KAHOOLAWE

MAUI

Hilo

HAWAII

Entered the Union
August 21, 1959

Hawaii

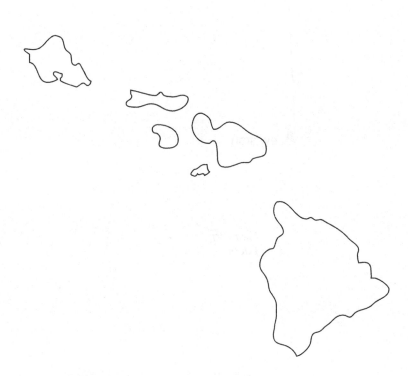

33

Idaho

Entered the Union
July 3, 1890

34

Idaho

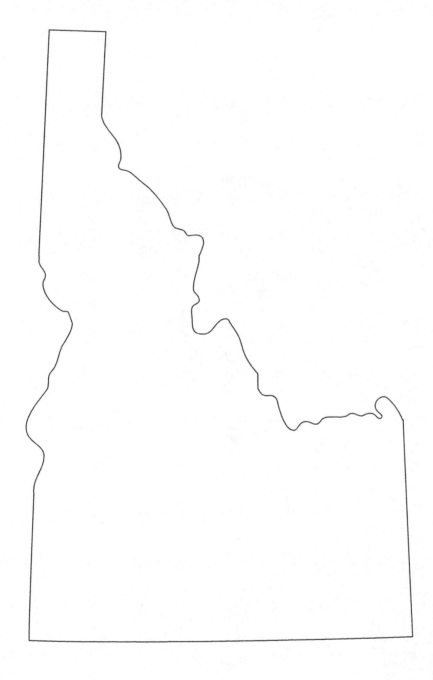

Illinois

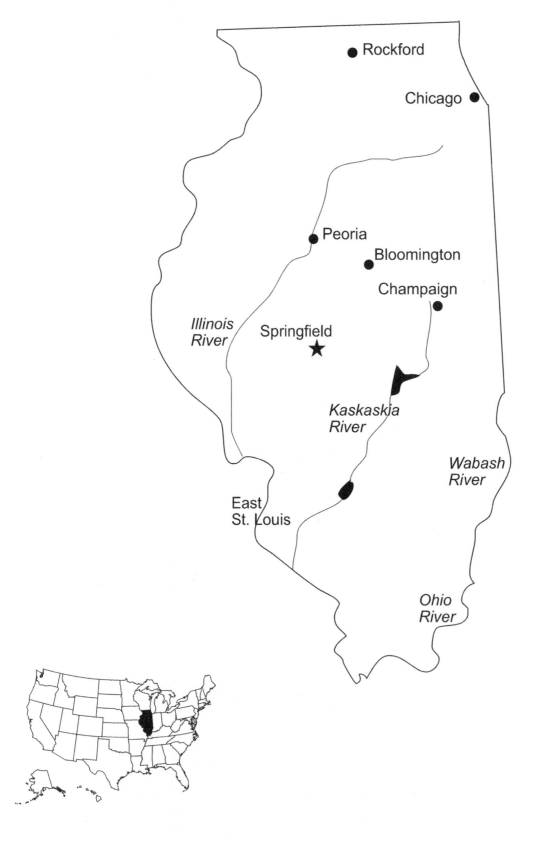

● Rockford

Chicago ●

● Peoria

Bloomington ●

Champaign ●

Illinois River

Springfield ★

Kaskaskia River

Wabash River

East St. Louis

Ohio River

Entered the Union
December 1, 1818

36

Illinois

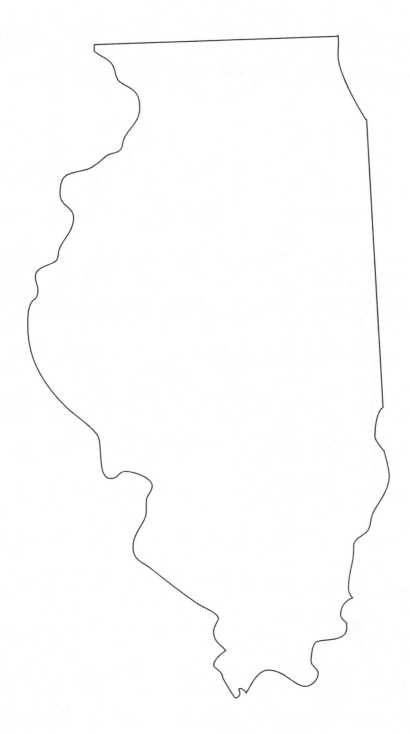

Indiana

South Bend

Gary

Fort Wayne

Wabash River

Indianapolis ★

Wabash River

Ohio River

White River

Evansville

Entered the Union
December 11, 1816

38

Indiana

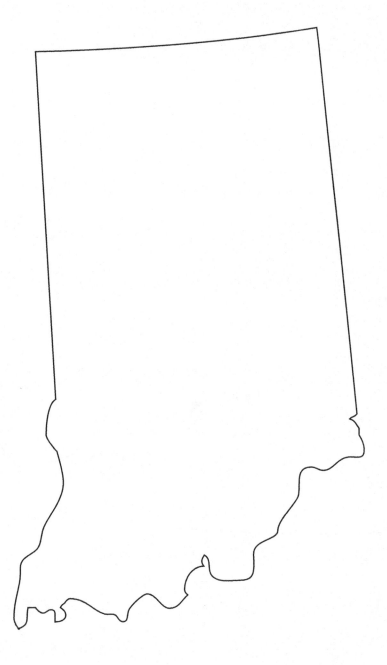

39

Iowa

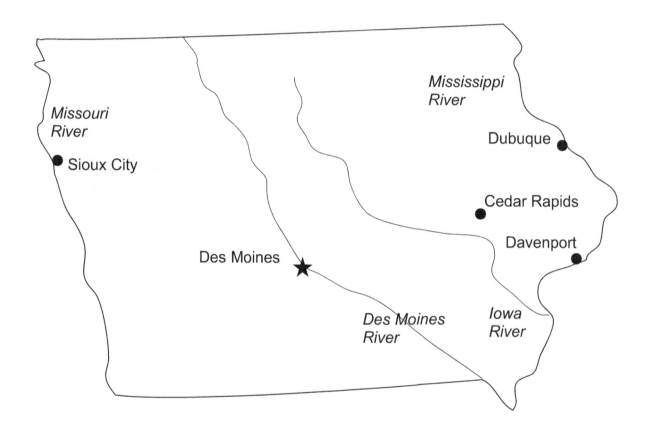

Missouri River

● Sioux City

Mississippi River

Dubuque ●

Cedar Rapids ●

Davenport ●

Des Moines ★

Des Moines River

Iowa River

Entered the Union
December 28, 1846

Iowa

41

Kansas

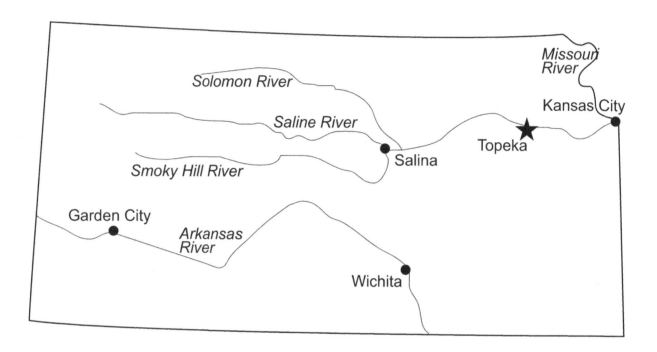

Missouri River

Solomon River

Saline River

Kansas City

Smoky Hill River

Topeka

Salina

Garden City

Arkansas River

Wichita

Entered the Union
January 29, 1861

Kansas

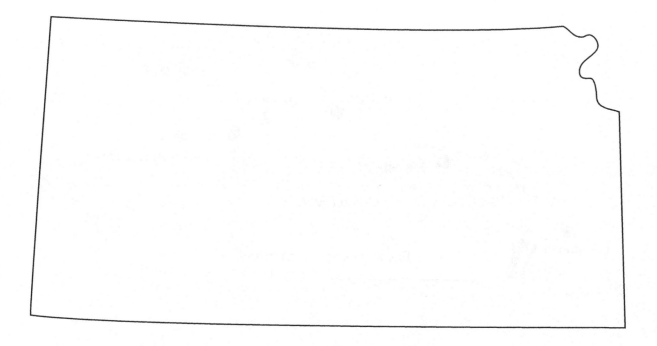

43

Kentucky

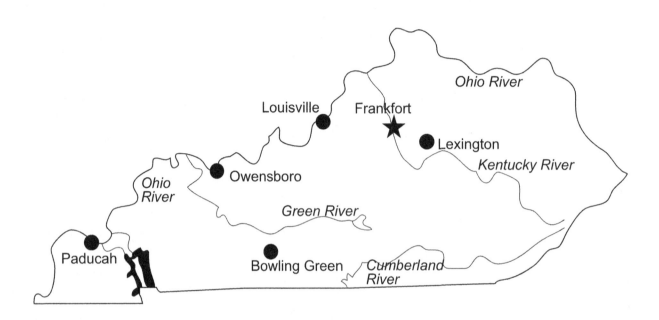

Louisville

Frankfort

Ohio River

Lexington

Kentucky River

Owensboro

Ohio River

Green River

Paducah

Bowling Green

Cumberland River

Entered the Union
June 1, 1792

44

Kentucky

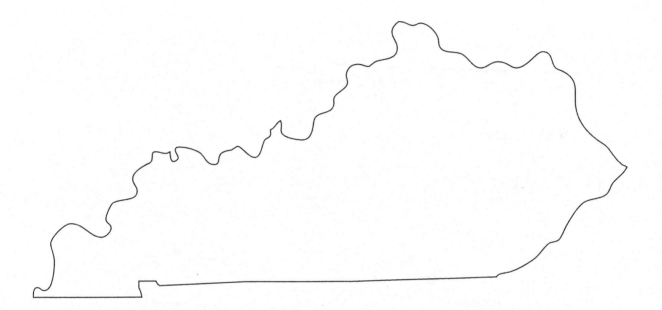

Louisiana

Shreveport

Mississippi
River

Red
River

Alexandria

Bundick
River

Mississippi
River

Baton Rouge
★

Lake
Pontchartrain

Lake Charles

New Orleans

Entered the Union
April 30, 1812

46

Louisiana

47

Maine

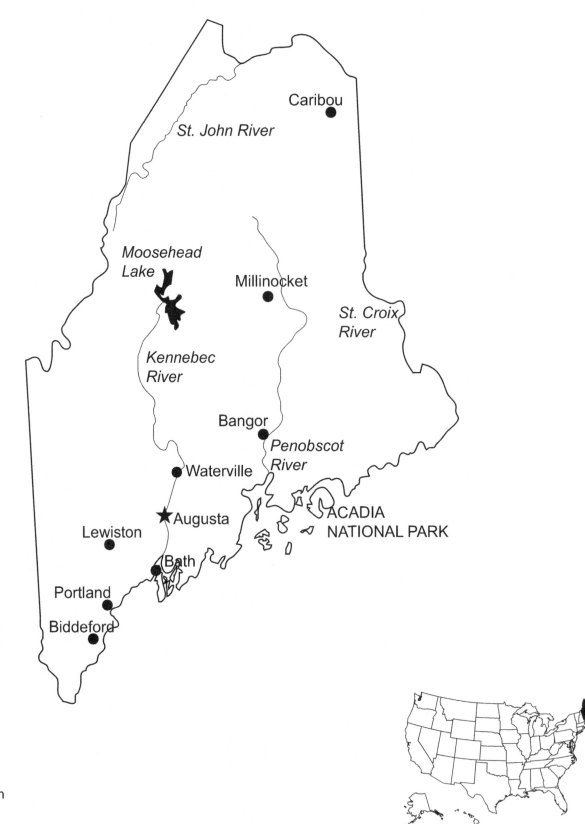

Caribou

St. John River

Moosehead Lake

Millinocket

St. Croix River

Kennebec River

Bangor

Penobscot River

Waterville

Augusta

ACADIA NATIONAL PARK

Lewiston

Bath

Portland

Biddeford

Entered the Union
March 15, 1820

48

Maine

Maryland

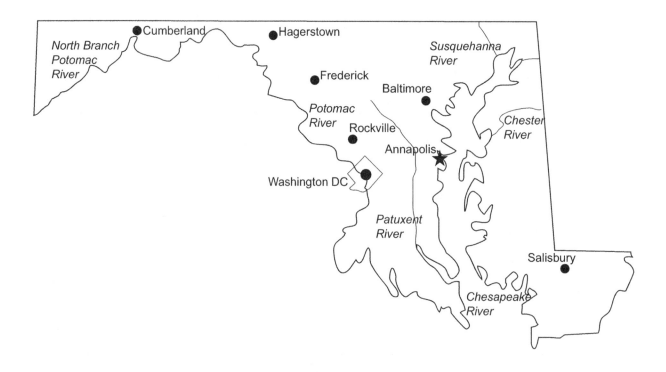

Cumberland

North Branch
Potomac
River

Hagerstown

Susquehanna
River

Frederick

Baltimore

Potomac
River

Chester
River

Rockville

Annapolis

Washington DC

Patuxent
River

Salisbury

Chesapeake
River

Entered the Union
April 28, 1788

Maryland

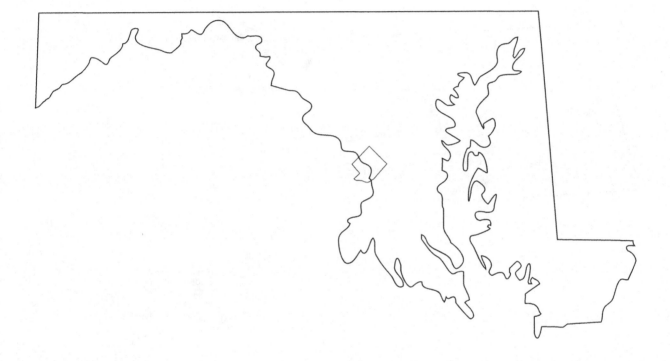

51

Massachusetts

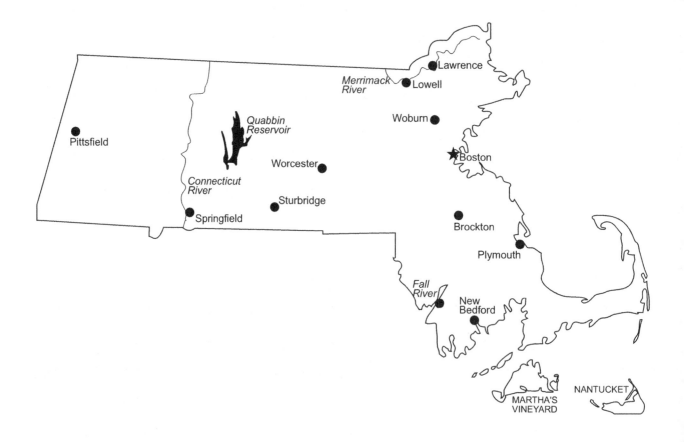

Lawrence

Merrimack River Lowell

Woburn

★Boston

Quabbin Reservoir

Worcester

Connecticut River

Sturbridge

Springfield

Brockton

Plymouth

Fall River

New Bedford

MARTHA'S VINEYARD

NANTUCKET

Pittsfield

Entered the Union
February 6, 1788

Massachusetts

Michigan

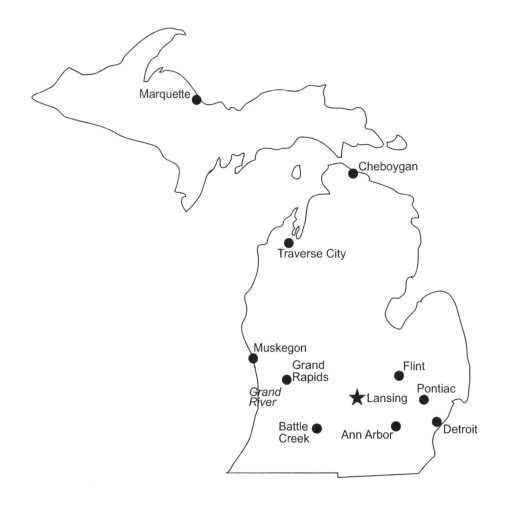

Marquette

Cheboygan

Traverse City

Muskegon

Grand
Rapids

Flint

*Grand
River*

⭐Lansing

Pontiac

Battle
Creek

Ann Arbor

Detroit

Entered the Union
January 26, 1837

Michigan

Minnesota

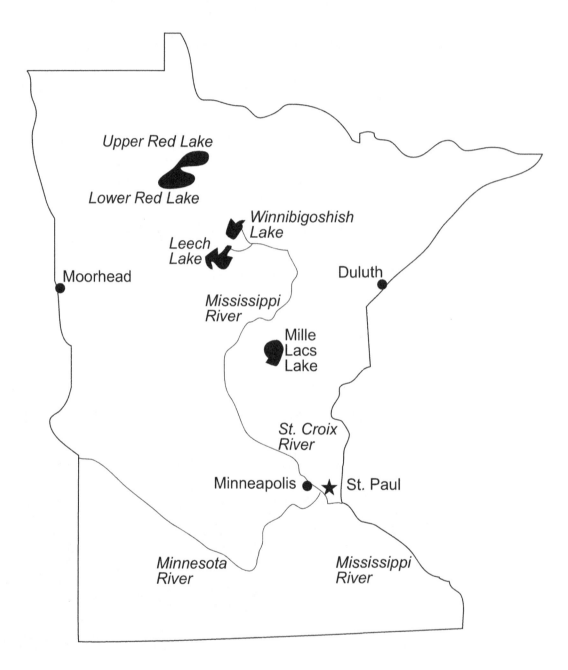

Upper Red Lake

Lower Red Lake

Winnibigoshish
Lake

Leech
Lake

Moorhead

Duluth

Mississippi
River

Mille
Lacs
Lake

St. Croix
River

Minneapolis ★ St. Paul

Minnesota
River

Mississippi
River

Entered the Union
May 11, 1858

Minnesota

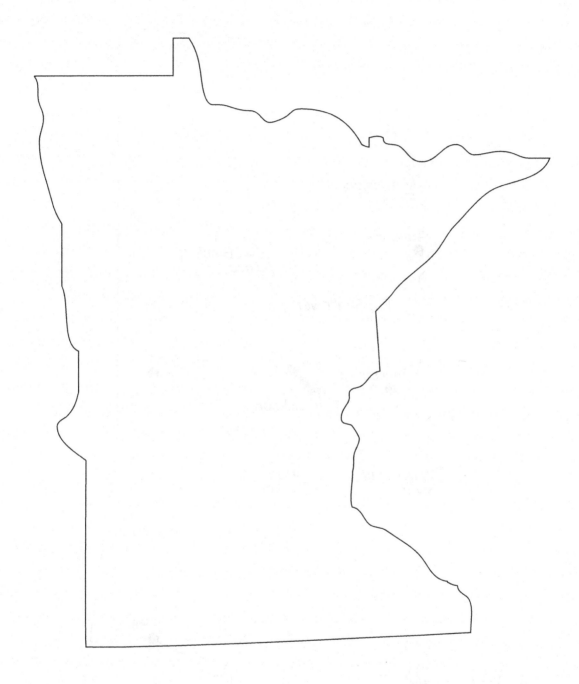

Mississippi

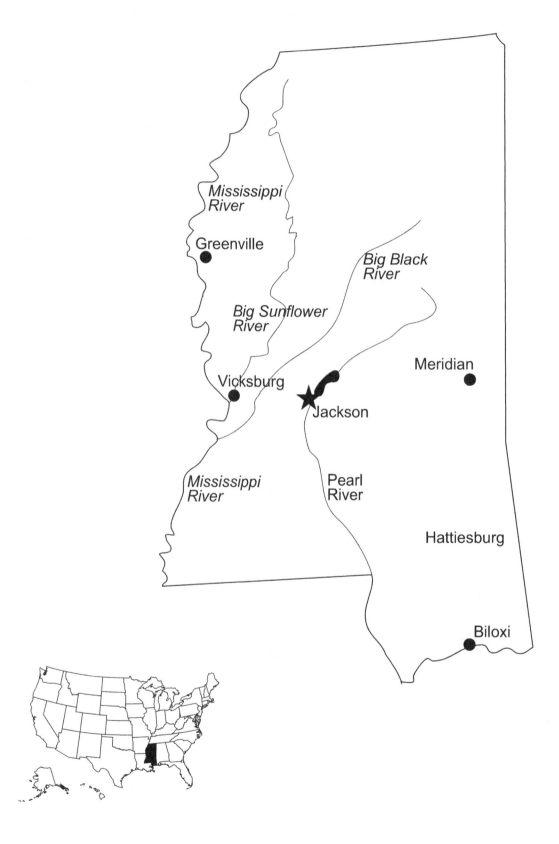

Greenville

Mississippi River

Big Black River

Big Sunflower River

Vicksburg

Meridian

★ Jackson

Mississippi River

Pearl River

Hattiesburg

Biloxi

Entered the Union
December 10, 1817

Mississippi

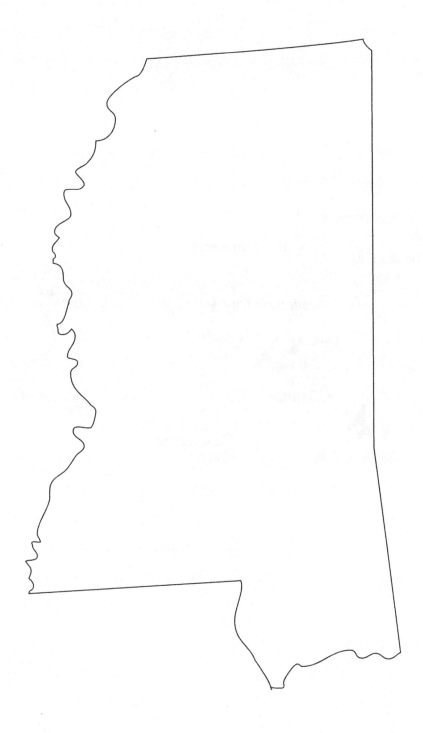

Missouri

Independence

Kansas City

Missouri River

Jefferson City ★

St. Louis

Osage River

Lake of the Ozarks

Springfield ●

Gasconade River

Mississippi River

Entered the Union
August 10, 1821

Missouri

Montana

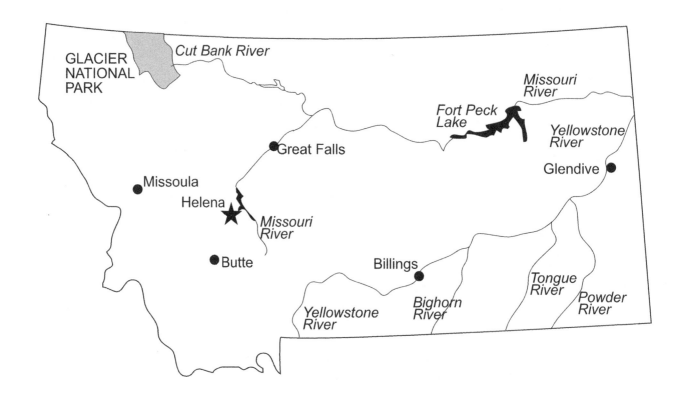

GLACIER NATIONAL PARK

Cut Bank River

Missouri River

Fort Peck Lake

Yellowstone River

●Great Falls

Glendive ●

●Missoula

Helena
★

Missouri River

●Butte

Billings ●

Tongue River

Powder River

Yellowstone River

Bighorn River

Entered the Union
November 8, 1889

Montana

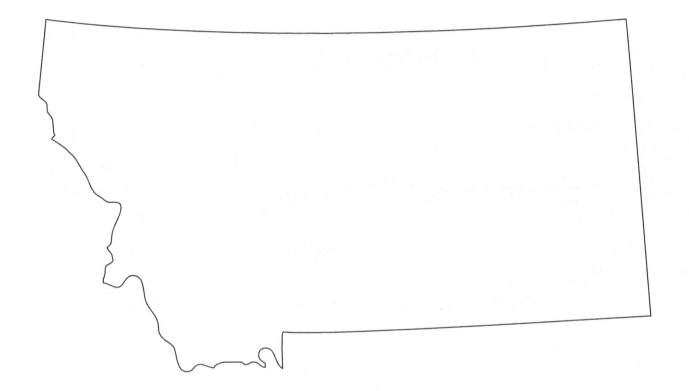

Nebraska

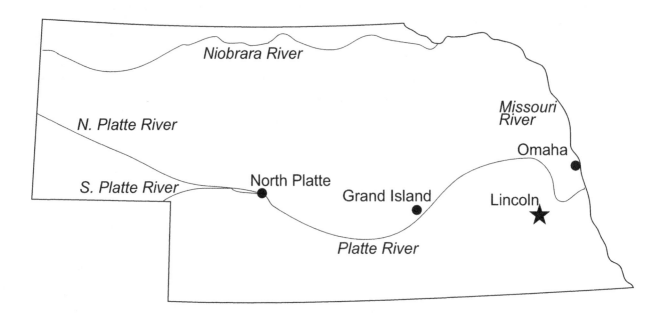

Niobrara River

N. Platte River

Missouri River

Omaha

S. Platte River

North Platte

Grand Island

Lincoln

Platte River

64

Entered the Union
March 1, 1867

Nebraska

65

Nevada

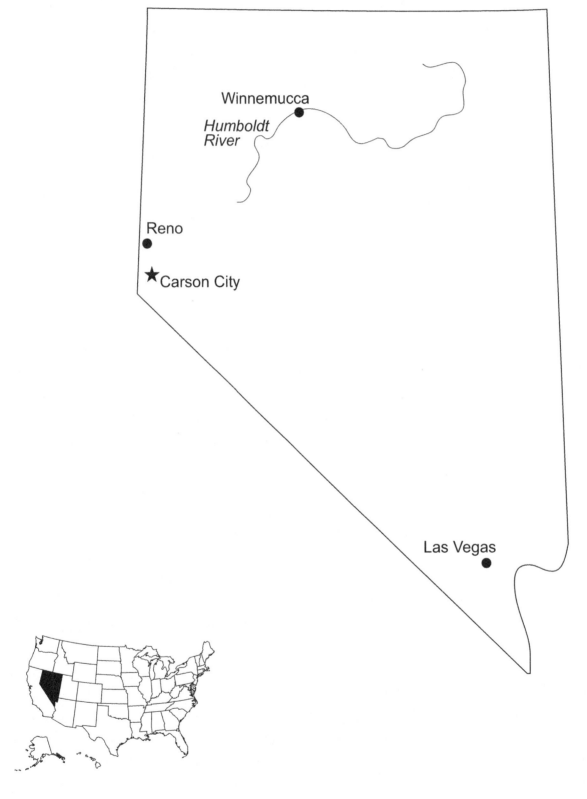

Winnemucca

Humboldt River

Reno

★Carson City

Las Vegas

Entered the Union
October 31, 1864

Nevada

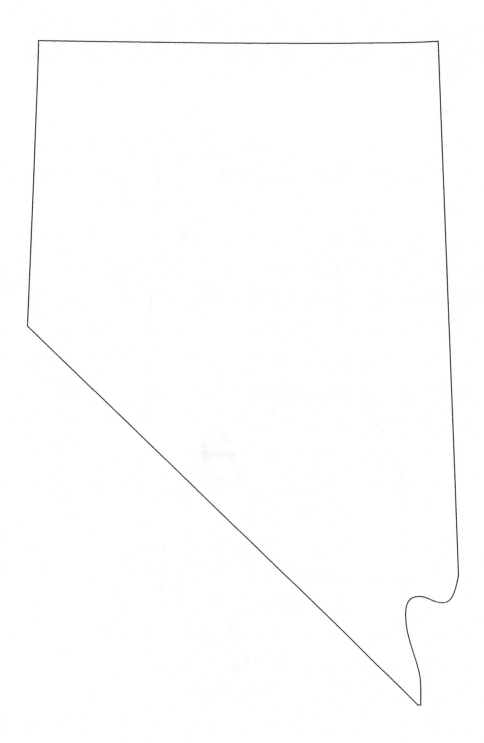

67

New Hampshire

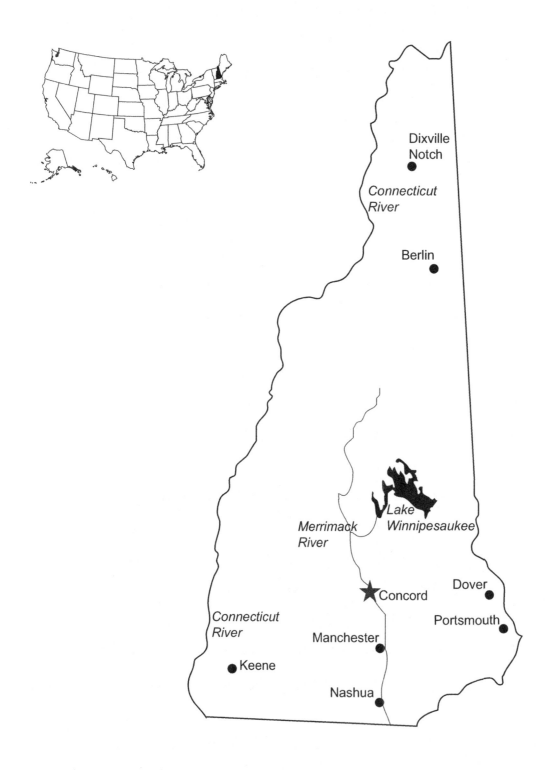

Dixville
Notch
●

*Connecticut
River*

Berlin
●

*Lake
Winnipesaukee*

*Merrimack
River*

Dover
★ Concord ●

*Connecticut
River*

Portsmouth
●

Manchester
●

● Keene

Nashua
●

Entered the Union
June 21, 1788

68

New Hampshire

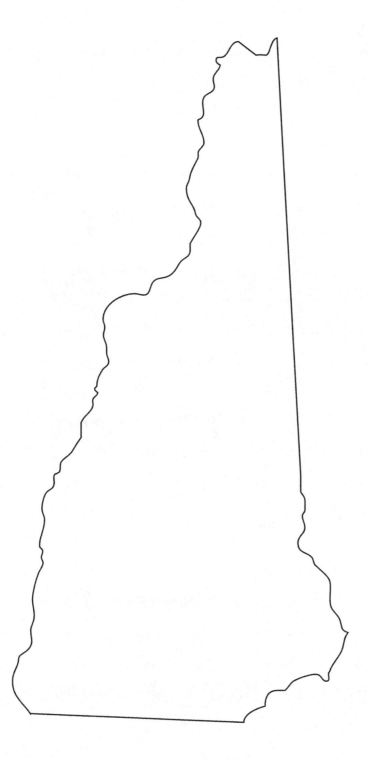

69

New Jersey

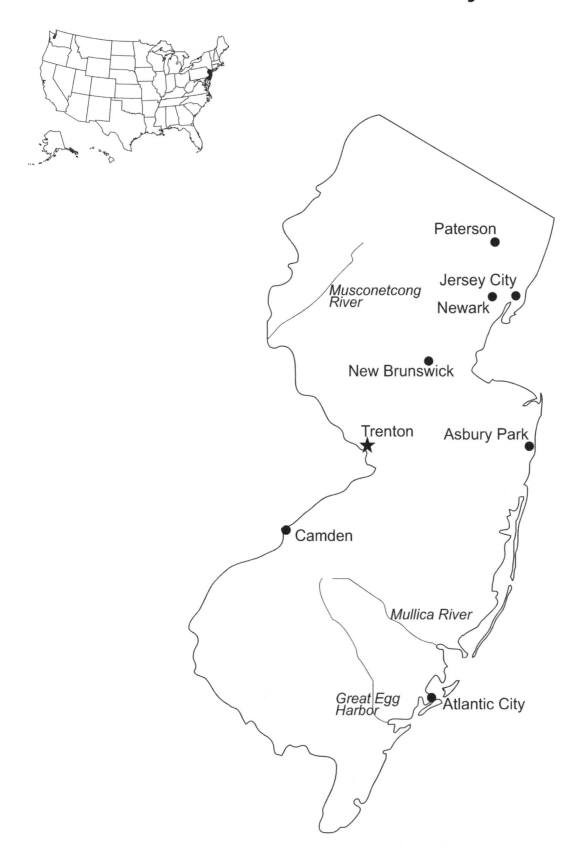

Paterson

Jersey City

Musconetcong River

Newark

New Brunswick

Trenton

Asbury Park

Camden

Mullica River

Great Egg Harbor

Atlantic City

Entered the Union
December 18, 1787

70

New Jersey

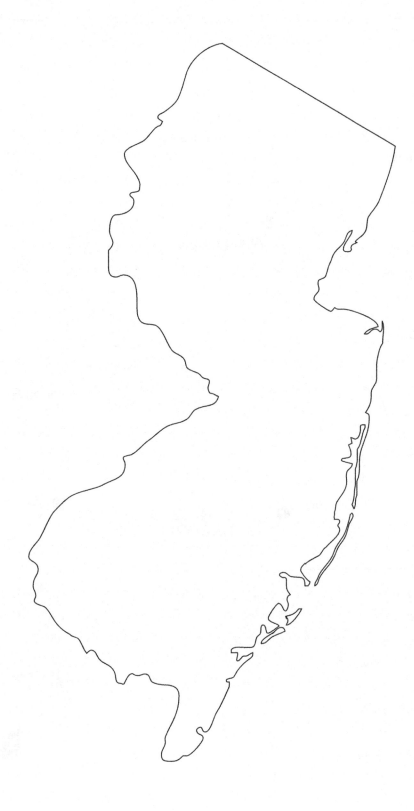

New Mexico

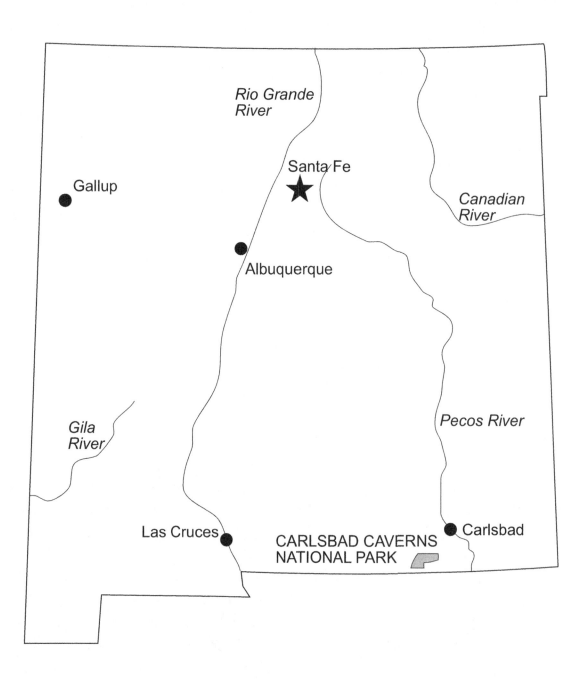

Rio Grande
River

Santa Fe
★

Gallup ●

Albuquerque ●

Canadian
River

Gila
River

Pecos River

Las Cruces ●

CARLSBAD CAVERNS
NATIONAL PARK

● Carlsbad

Entered the Union
January 6, 1912

New Mexico

New York

Watertown

Oswego

Erie Canal Rochester

Buffalo Syracuse

Schenectady

Albany

Ithaca

Hudson
River

Binghamton

New York City

Entered the Union
July 26, 1788

New York

75

North Carolina

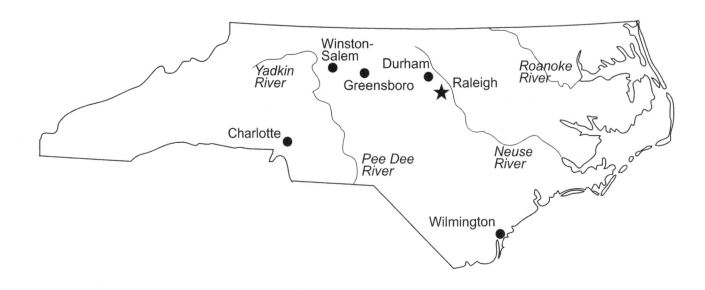

Winston-Salem

Yadkin River

Durham

Greensboro

Raleigh

Roanoke River

Charlotte

Pee Dee River

Neuse River

Wilmington

Entered the Union
November 21, 1789

North Carolina

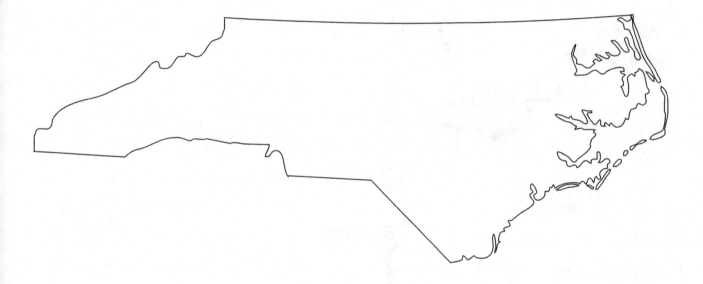

North Dakota

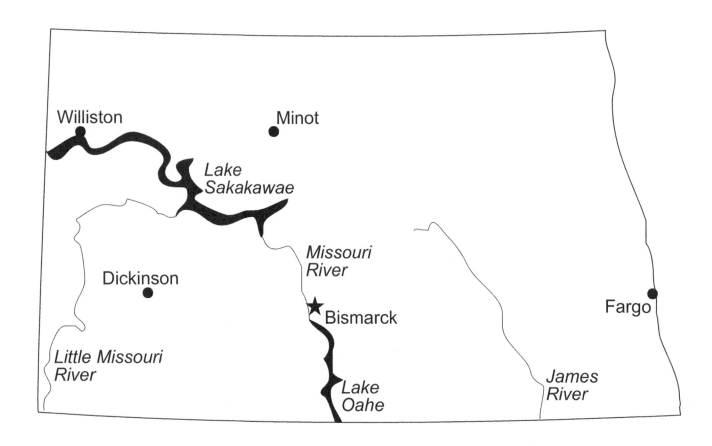

Williston

Minot

*Lake
Sakakawae*

*Missouri
River*

Dickinson

Fargo

*Little Missouri
River*

★ Bismarck

*Lake
Oahe*

*James
River*

Entered the Union
November 2, 1889

North Dakota

Ohio

Toledo

Cleveland

Akron

Canton

Great Miami River

★ Columbus

Ohio River

Dayton

Muskingum River

Cincinnati

Ohio River

Entered the Union
March 1, 1803

Ohio

81

Oklahoma

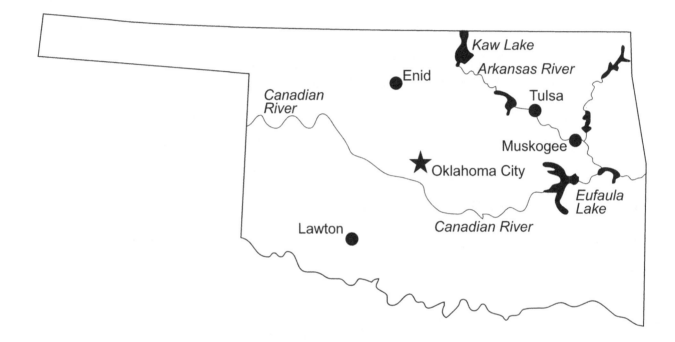

Kaw Lake

Enid

Canadian River

Arkansas River

Tulsa

Muskogee

★ Oklahoma City

Eufaula Lake

Canadian River

Lawton

Entered the Union
November 16, 1907

Oklahoma

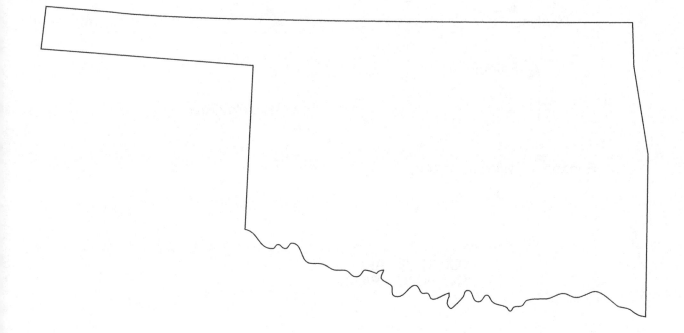

83

Oregon

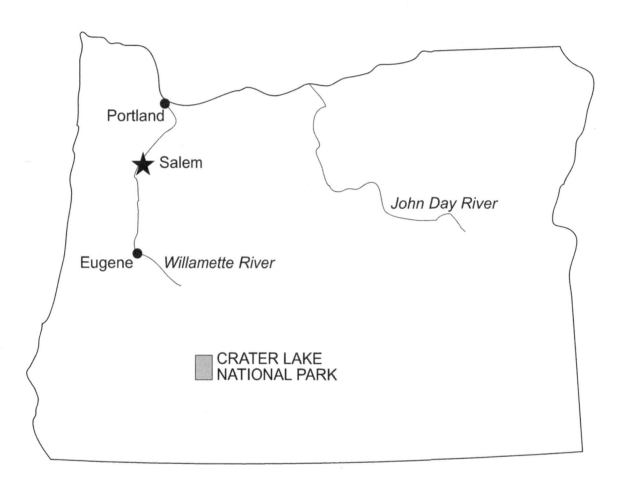

Portland

Salem

John Day River

Eugene *Willamette River*

CRATER LAKE
NATIONAL PARK

Entered the Union
February 14, 1859

Oregon

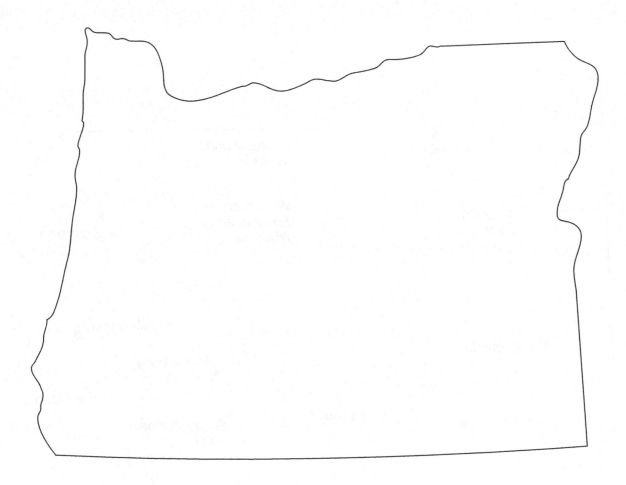

Pennsylvania

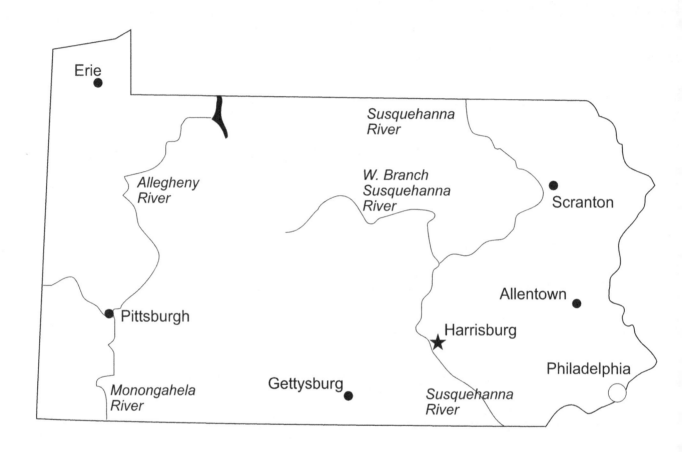

Erie

Susquehanna
River

W. Branch
Susquehanna
River

Scranton

Allegheny
River

Allentown

Pittsburgh

Harrisburg

Philadelphia

Gettysburg

Monongahela
River

Susquehanna
River

Entered the Union
December 12, 1787

Pennsylvania

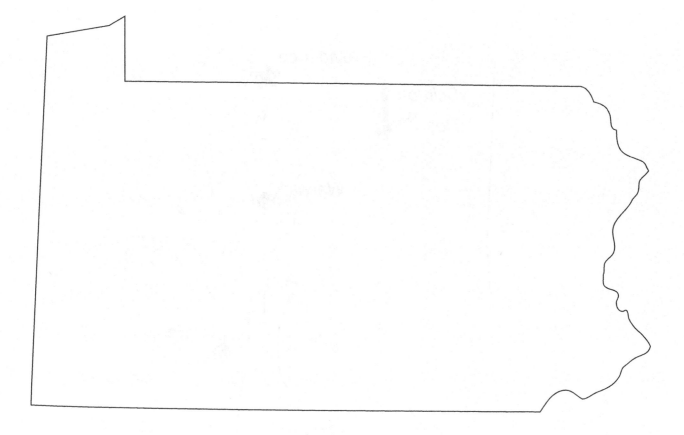

Rhode Island

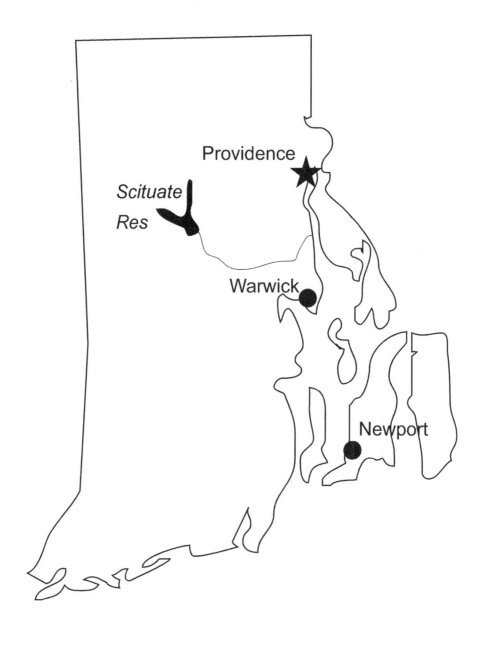

Providence

Scituate
Res

Warwick

Newport

Entered the Union
May 29, 1790

Rhode Island

South Carolina

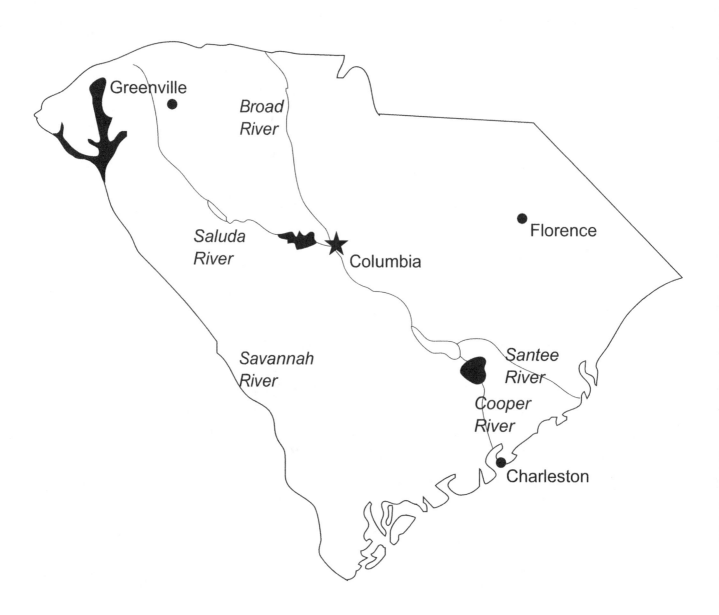

Greenville

Broad River

Saluda River

★ Columbia

● Florence

Savannah River

Santee River

Cooper River

● Charleston

Entered the Union
May 23, 1788

South Carolina

South Dakota

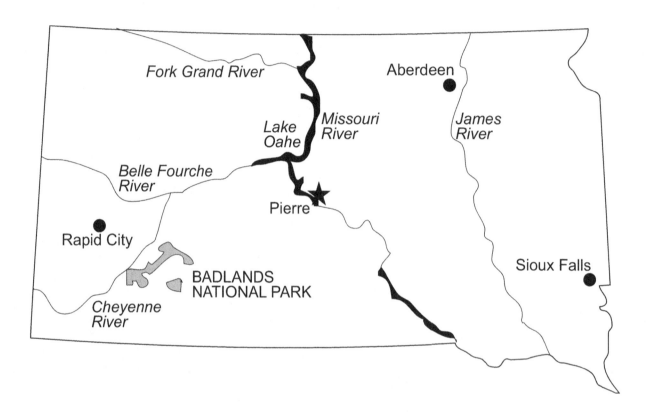

Fork Grand River

Aberdeen

Lake
Oahe

Missouri
River

James
River

Belle Fourche
River

Pierre

Rapid City

Sioux Falls

BADLANDS
NATIONAL PARK

Cheyenne
River

Entered the Union
November 2, 1889

92

South Dakota

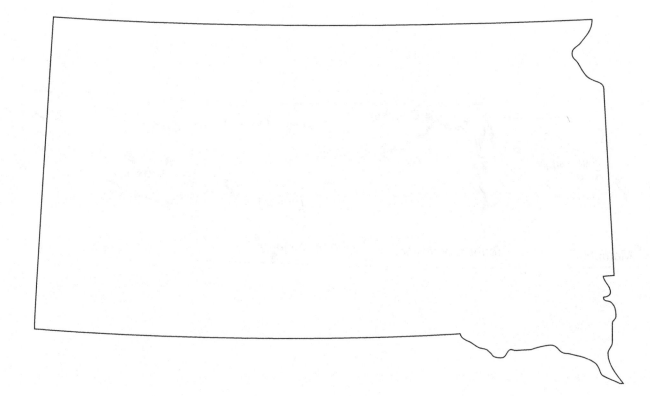

Tennessee

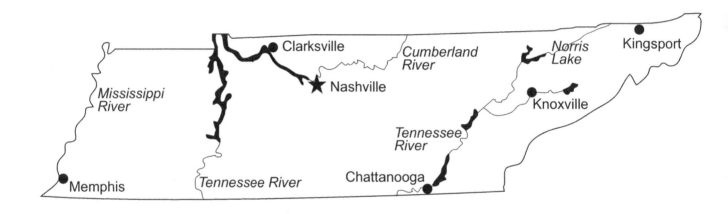

Clarksville
Cumberland River
Nashville
Mississippi River
Norris Lake
Kingsport
Knoxville
Tennessee River
Tennessee River
Chattanooga
Memphis

Entered the Union
June 1, 1796

Tennessee

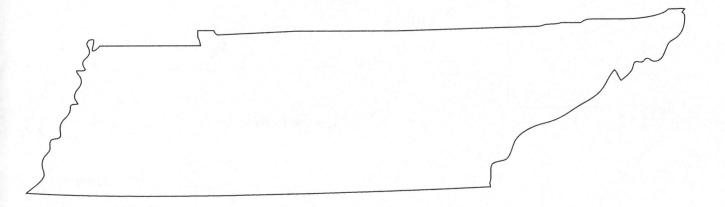

Texas

Amarillo

Red River

Brazos River

Lubbock

Fort Worth   Dallas

Arlington

El Paso

Colorado River

Beaumont

Austin

Houston

Pecos River

San Antonio

Rio Grande

Corpus Christi

Rio Grande

Entered the Union
December 29, 1845

96

Texas

Utah

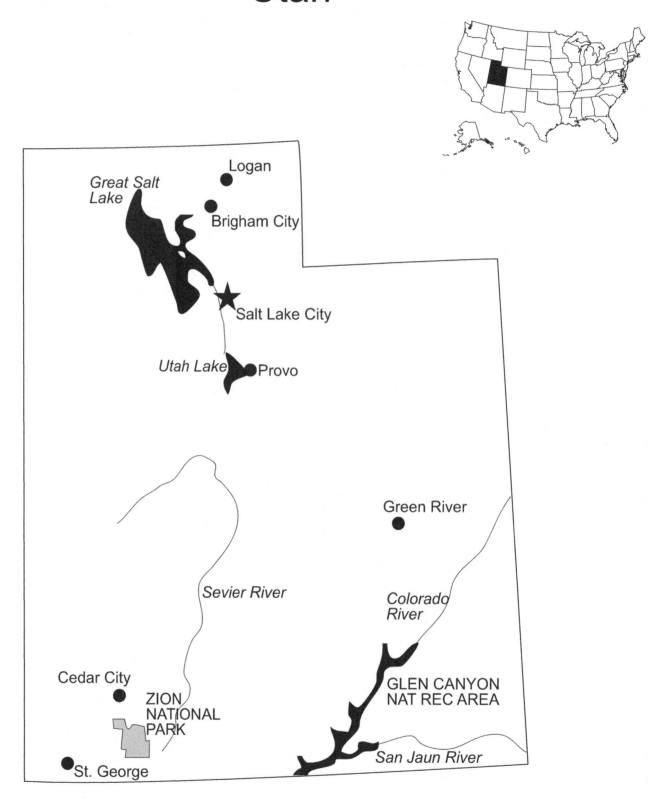

Logan

Great Salt Lake

Brigham City

Salt Lake City

Utah Lake Provo

Green River

Sevier River

Colorado River

Cedar City

ZION NATIONAL PARK

GLEN CANYON NAT REC AREA

St. George

San Jaun River

Entered the Union
January 4, 1896

Utah

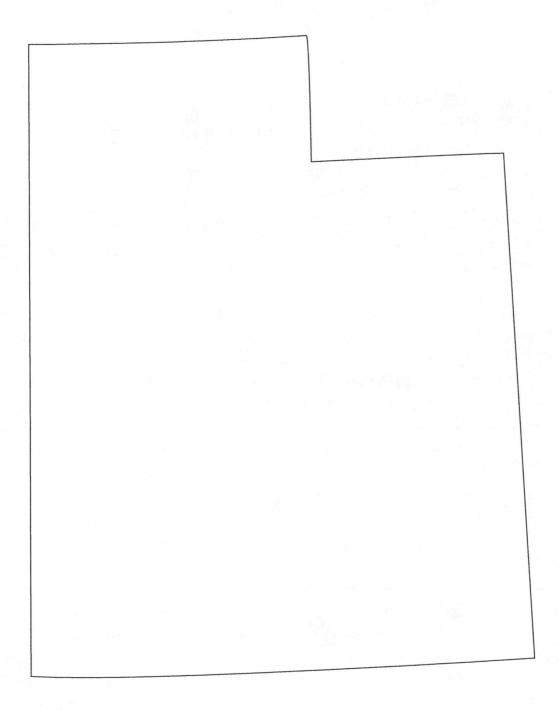

Vermont

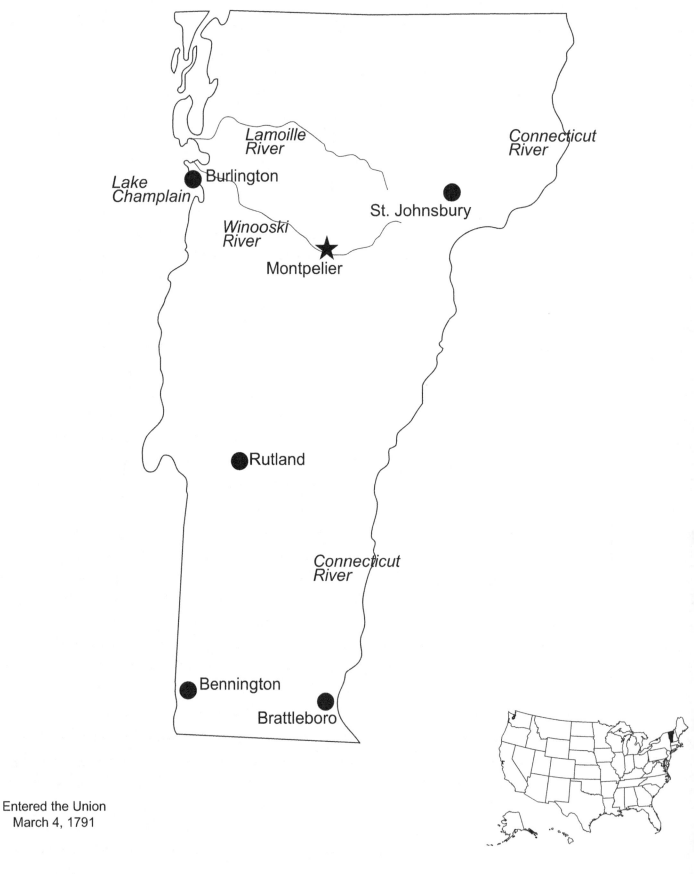

Lamoille River

Connecticut River

Lake Champlain

Burlington

St. Johnsbury

Winooski River

★ Montpelier

Rutland

Connecticut River

Bennington

Brattleboro

Entered the Union
March 4, 1791

Vermont

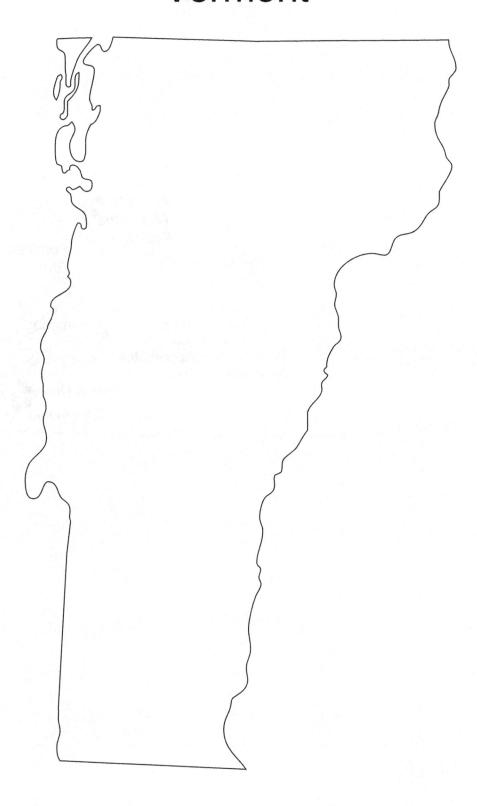

101

Virginia

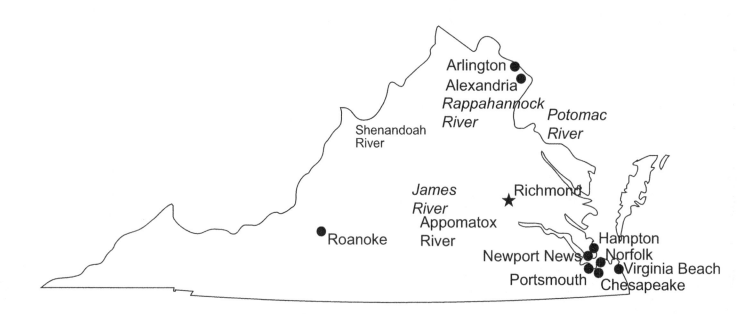

Arlington
Alexandria
Rappahannock River
Shenandoah River
Potomac River

James River
Richmond
Appomatox River
Roanoke

Hampton
Newport News
Norfolk
Portsmouth
Virginia Beach
Chesapeake

Entered the Union
June 25, 1788

Virginia

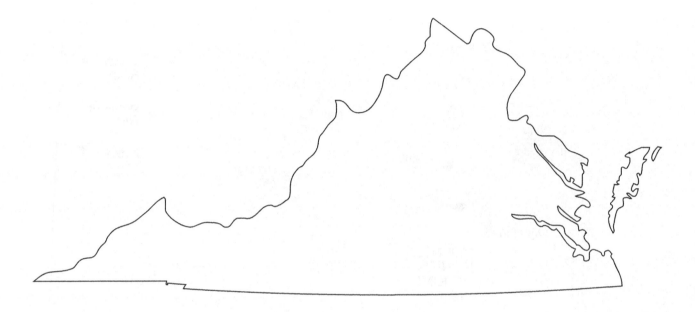

Washington

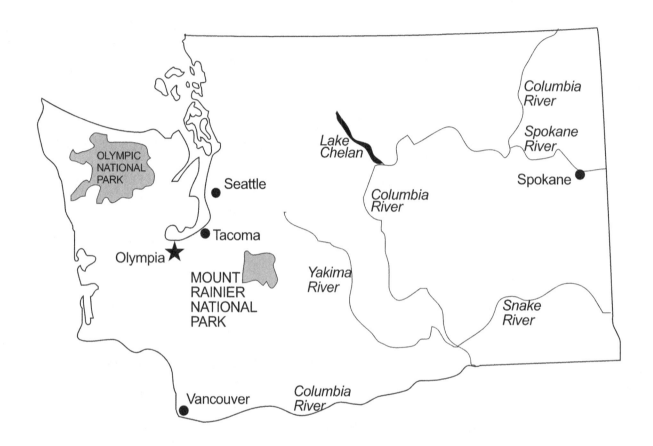

OLYMPIC NATIONAL PARK

Seattle

Tacoma

Olympia

MOUNT RAINIER NATIONAL PARK

Vancouver

Lake Chelan

Columbia River

Columbia River

Yakima River

Columbia River

Spokane River

Columbia River

Spokane

Snake River

Entered the Union
November 11, 1889

Washington

West Virginia

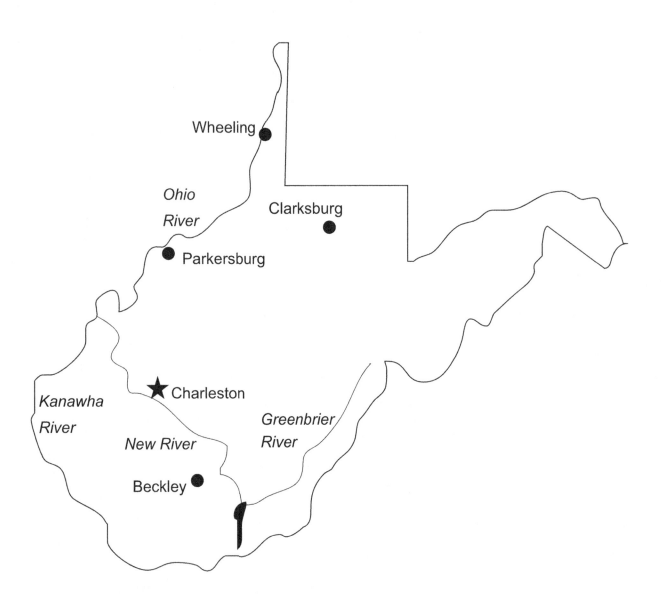

Wheeling ●

Ohio
River

Clarksburg ●

● Parkersburg

★ Charleston

Kanawha
River

Greenbrier
River

New River

Beckley ●

Entered the Union
June 20, 1863

106

West Virginia

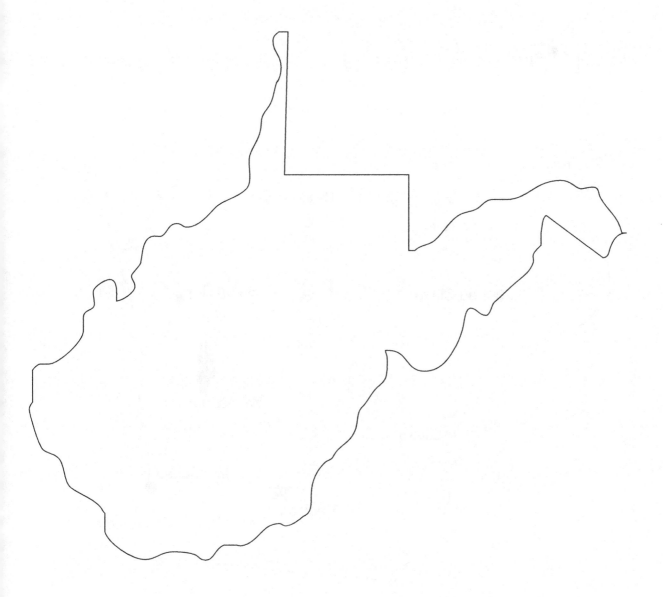

Wisconsin

Entered the Union
May 29, 1848

Wisconsin

Wyoming

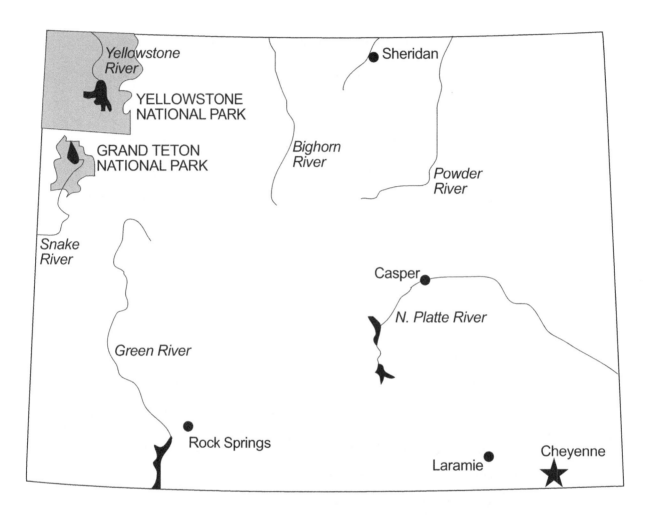

Yellowstone River

YELLOWSTONE NATIONAL PARK

GRAND TETON NATIONAL PARK

Snake River

Bighorn River

Sheridan

Powder River

Green River

Casper

N. Platte River

Rock Springs

Laramie

Cheyenne

Entered the Union
July 10, 1890

Wyoming

Northern Mariana Islands and Guam

Farallon
De Pajaros
Maug Islands
∘ Asungion

∘ Agrihan

∂ Pagam
∘ Alamagan
· Guguam
∘ Sarigan
Anatahan ∘
∘ Farallon
De Medinilla

Tinian ∘ Saipan
Aguijam
∘ Rota
∘ Guam

Mariana Trench

Guam

Capital:	Hagatna (Agana)
Population:	178,000
Size:	209 sq mi
Territory:	Guam Organic Act of 1950, unincorporated organized territory of the United States
Motto:	Where America's Day Begins
Bird:	Marianas Rose Crown Fruit Dove
Flower:	Bougainvillea Spectabilis
Tree:	Ifil Tree
Fun Fact:	Guam was discovered by sea-faring people who migrated from Southeast Asia around 4000 BC, western contact was by Ferdinand Magellan in 1521.

Guam

★ Hagatna (Agana)

Saipan

Capital Hill ★
● Garapan

Chalan ●
Kanoa

Northern Mariana Islands and Guam

Commonwealth of the Northern
Mariana Islands

Capital:	Saipan
Population:	53,883
Size	179 sq mi
Territory	1976 Covenant to Establish a Commonwealth of the Northern Mariana Islands (CNMI) in Political Union with the United States.
Bird:	Mariana Fruit Dove
Flower:	Plumeria Flower
Tree:	Flame Tree
Fun Fact:	There are active volcanoes on the islands of Anatahan, Pagan and Agrihan

Guam

Saipan

Puerto Rico

San Juan

Aguadilla

Arecibo

● Bayamon

Culebra Island

Mayaguez

Humacao

Ponce

Guayama

Vieques Island

Ceded to the Union
December 10, 1898

Puerto Rico

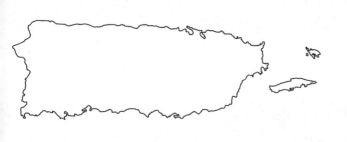

Capital:	San Juan
Population:	3,706,690
Size:	9,104 sq mi
Sovereignty:	December 10, 1898 from Kingdom of Spain
Motto:	John is His Name
Nickname:	Isle of Enchantment
Bird:	Stripe-headed Tanager
Flower:	Puerto Rican Hibiscus
Tree:	Silk-Cotton Tree
Fun Fact:	Puerto Rico was discovered by Christopher Columbus

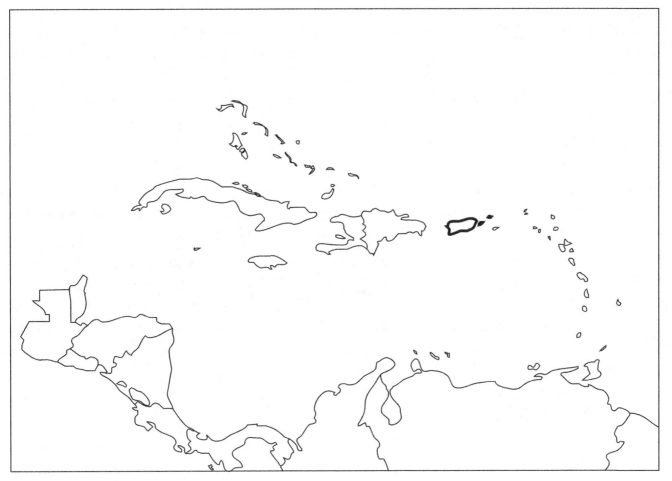

United States Virgin Islands

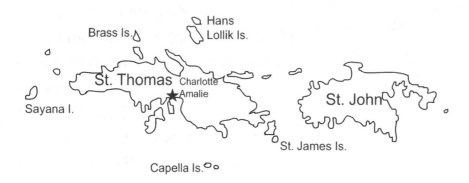

Brass Is.

Hans
Lollik Is.

St. Thomas

Charlotte
Amalie

Sayana I.

St. John

St. James Is.

Capella Is.

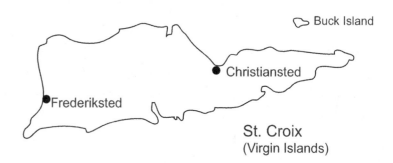

Buck Island

Christiansted

Frederiksted

St. Croix
(Virgin Islands)

US Takes Possession
March 31, 1917

United States Virgin Islands

Capital: Charlotte Amalie, St. Thomas Island
Population: 109,750
Size: 133 sq mi
Territory: 1916, Treaty of the Danish West Indies, organized,
                      unincorporated United States Territory, organized
                      under the Revised Organic Act of 1954
Motto: United in Pride and Hope
Bird: Yellow Breast
Flower: Yellow Elder
Fun Fact: U.S. Virgin Islands is made up of 60 to 70 islands

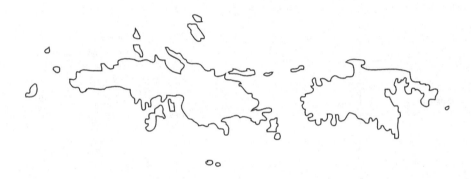

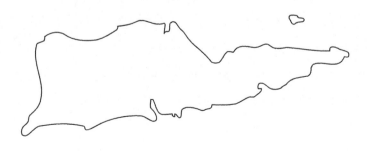

North America

118

North America

Juneau

North America

World-Robinson Projection

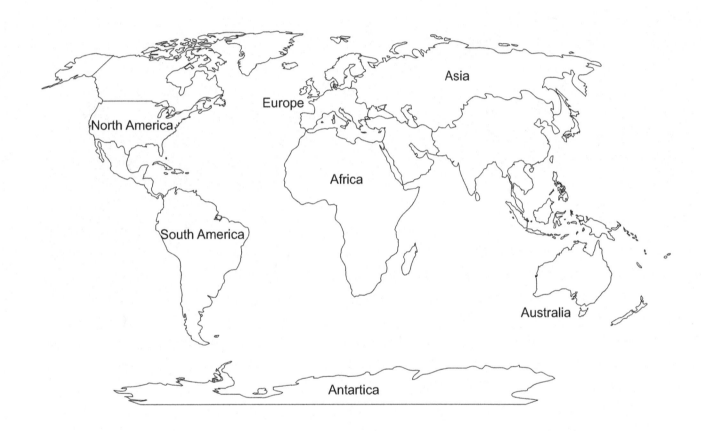

North America

Europe

Asia

Africa

South America

Australia

Antartica

World-Robinson Projection

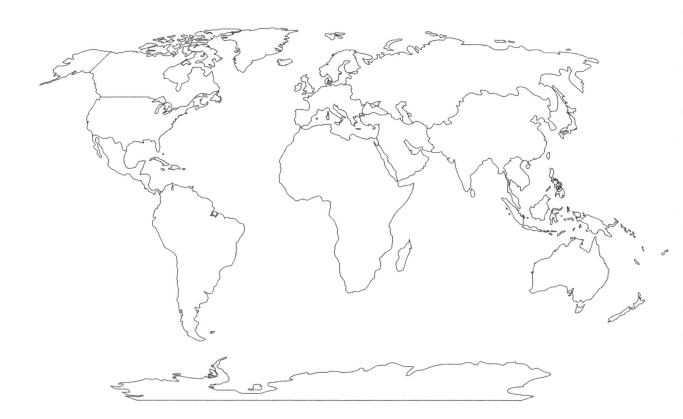

122

World — Mercator Projection

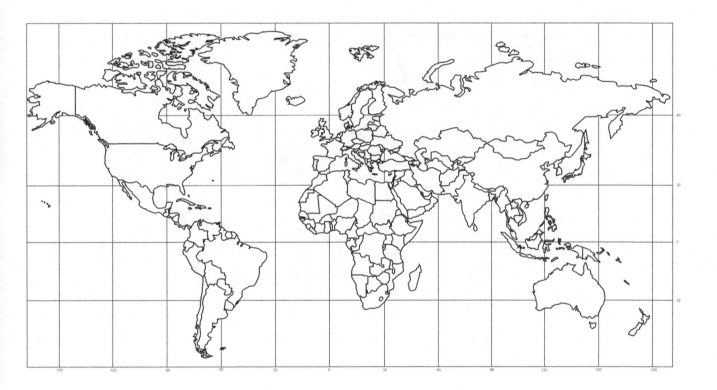

World — Mercator Projection

World Map — Mercator Projection

125

Check Out All Our Map Books

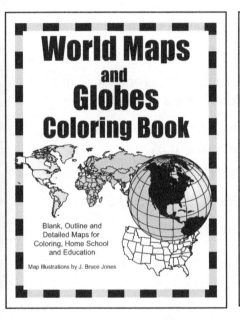

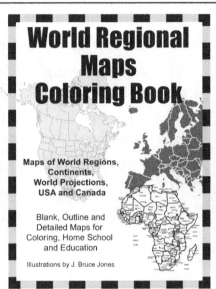

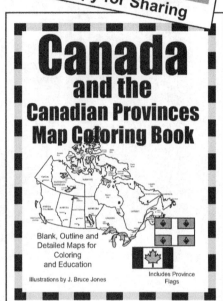

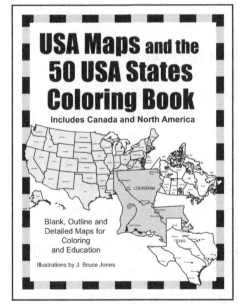

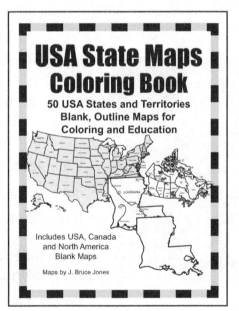

Blank, Outline and Detailed Maps for Coloring, Homeschool and Education

Made in USA

Blank, Outline, Printable PDF Map Sets and Editable Clip Art Maps

Perfect for Education, Home and School

Individual, Blank, Printable, Outline PDF Map Sets Your Students Can Trace and Color

- Learn geography, add names and features.
- Create lessons, games, in-class quizzes, study aids.
- Help your students learn the names and location of the states, countries, world regions and more.
- Students can trace the outlines of the blank maps, highlight continents and countries.
- Each map is an individual PDF file that can be printed out.
- USA, States, Canada, World Regions and Globes
- **A great teaching resource**

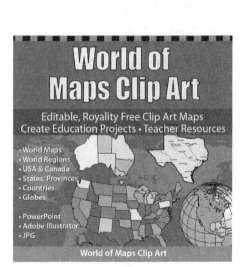

World of Maps Clip Art

Our Digital Map Collection includes all our easy to edit, royalty free, PowerPoint and Adobe Illustrator clip art maps. Plus a jpg version of every map.

- Editable Maps in PowerPoint and Adobe Illustrator
- PowerPoint maps also work in Keynote and Google Slides
- Have the entire collection at your finger tips.

Perfect for educational projects, teacher resources, scrapbooking, graphic design.

- Great for homeschool, education, or home decor images and posters.
- Each PowerPoint or Illustrator country, state or world map can be colored, and customized. Text can be edited or added.

Visit www.FreeUSandWorldMaps.com

Made in the USA
Las Vegas, NV
22 March 2024

87614269R00072